How to Draw a NINJA for Kids

Author Tony R. Smith

Copyright © 2019 by Tony R. Smith. All Rights Reserved.

No part of this publication may be reproduced, distributed, or transmitted in any form or by any means, including photocopying, recording, or other electronic or mechanical methods, or by any information storage and retrieval system without the prior written permission of Smith Show Publishing, except in the case of very brief quotations embodied in critical reviews and certain other noncommercial uses permitted by copyright law.

First, Look at our final drawing.

Step 1. Complete our drawing.

Step 2. Look at your final drawing.

Step 3. Sketch/Draw your own Ninja Warrior.

 How to Draw a Ninja

 First, Look at our final drawing.

 Step 1. Complete our drawing.

 Step 2. Look at your final drawing.

 Step 3. Sketch/Draw your own Ninja Warrior.

Complete the Drawing

Sketch/Draw

Complete the Drawing

Sketch/Draw

Complete the Drawing

Sketch/Draw

Complete the Drawing

Sketch/Draw

Sketch/Draw

Complete the Drawing

Sketch/Draw

Complete the Drawing

Sketch/Draw

Sketch/Draw

Complete the Drawing

Sketch/Draw

Sketch/Draw

Sketch/Draw

Sketch/Draw

Sketch/Draw

Complete the Drawing

Sketch/Draw

Sketch/Draw

Complete the Drawing

Sketch/Draw

Complete the Drawing

Sketch/Draw

Complete the Drawing

Sketch/Draw

Sketch/Draw

Complete the Drawing

Sketch/Draw

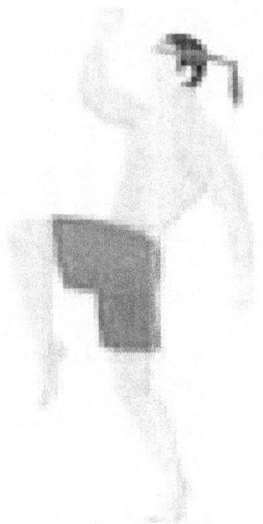
MUAY THAI

NINJUTSU

AIKIDO

BOXING

Sketch/Draw

Bonus

Complete the Drawing

Sketch/Draw

Bonus

Complete the Drawing

Sketch/Draw

Bonus

Complete the Drawing

Sketch/Draw

Bonus

Complete the Drawing

Sketch/Draw

Bonus

Complete the Drawing

Sketch/Draw

Bonus

Sketch/Draw

Bonus

Complete the Drawing

Sketch/Draw

Bonus

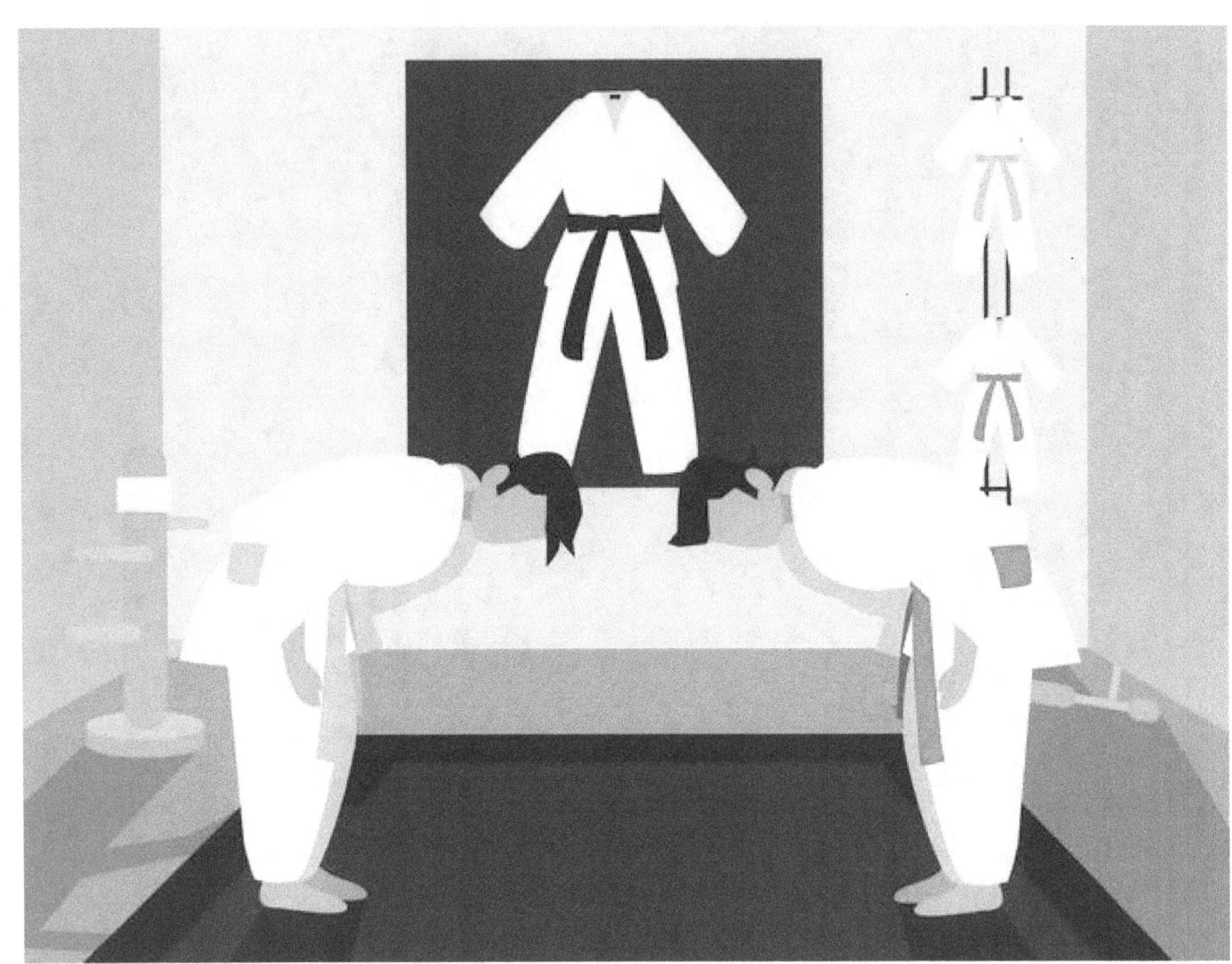

Sketch/Draw

Bonus

Sketch/Draw

Bonus

Sketch/Draw

Bonus

Sketch/Draw

Bonus

Sketch/Draw

Sketch/Draw

Sketch/Draw

Sketch/Draw

Sketch/Draw

Bonus

Sketch/Draw

Sketch/Draw

Sketch/Draw

Sketch/Draw

Sketch/Draw

www.ingramcontent.com/pod-product-compliance
Lightning Source LLC
Chambersburg PA
CBHW081727100526
44591CB00016B/2527